The Poetry of William Carlos Williams

Volume I - Sour Grapes & The Tempers

William Carlos Williams was born on September 17, 1883 in Rutherford, New Jersey.

As well as being a poet he painted and maintained a lifelong interest in it. Williams was also a physician in both paediatrics and general medicine. He served at the Passaic General Hospital in Passaic, New Jersey as chief of paediatrics from 1924 until his death.

Williams is most well-known for his poems that are closely associated with the Modernism and Imagism movements. In addition to poetry he occasionally wrote short stories, plays, novels, essays, and worked on translations.

He practiced medicine by day and wrote at night. Early in his career, he briefly became involved in the Imagist movement via friendships with Ezra Pound and Hilda Doolittle (H.D.). Soon his opinions moved away from theirs and his style began to confirm his alignment to a modernist expression of his surrounding environment.

From the late 40's health became a major issue in his life but with himself as the patient. He suffered a heart attack in 1948 and, after 1949, a series of strokes.

One such stoke in 1953 left him in hospital for four months and brought about severe depression.

In these later years, Williams mentored and influenced many younger poets especially the American literary movements of the 1950s; the Beat movement, the San Francisco Renaissance, the Black Mountain school, and the New York School.

One of Williams's most productive relationships was with fellow New Jersey poet Allen Ginsberg. Williams included several of Ginsberg's letters in Paterson, stating that one of them helped inspire the fifth volume of that work. Williams also wrote the introduction to Ginsberg's Howl and Other Poems in 1956.

William Carlos Williams died on March 4th, 1963, at the age of 79 at his home in Rutherford. He was buried in Hillside Cemetery in Lyndhurst, New Jersey.

Index of Poems

SOUR GRAPES

THE LATE SINGER

Here it is spring again
and I still a young man!
I am late at my singing.
The sparrow with the black rain on his breast
has been at his cadenzas for two weeks past:
What is it that is dragging at my heart?
The grass by the back door
is stiff with sap.
The old maples are opening
their branches of brown and yellow moth-flowers.
A moon hangs in the blue
in the early afternoons over the marshes.
I am late at my singing.

MARCH

I
Winter is long in this climate
and spring a matter of a few days
only, a flower or two picked
from mud or from among wet leaves
or at best against treacherous
bitterness of wind, and sky shining
teasingly, then closing in black
and sudden, with fierce jaws.

II
March,

you remind me of
the pyramids, our pyramids
stript of the polished stone
that used to guard them!
March,
you are like Fra Angelico
at Fiesole, painting on plaster!

March,
you are like a band of
young poets that have not learned
the blessedness of warmth
(or have forgotten it).

At any rate
I am moved to write poetry
for the warmth there is in it
and for the loneliness
a poem that shall have you
in it March.

III
See!
Ashur-ban-i-pal,
the archer king, on horse-back,
in blue and yellow enamel!
with drawn bow facing lions
standing on their hind legs,
fangs bared! his shafts
bristling in their necks!

Sacred bulls dragons
in embossed brickwork
marching in four tiers
along the sacred way to
Nebuchadnezzar's throne hall!
They shine in the sun,
they that have been marching
marching under the dust of
ten thousand dirt years.

Now
they are coming into bloom again!
See them!
marching still, bared by
the storms from my calendar
winds that blow back the sand!
winds that enfilade dirt!
winds that by strange craft
have whipt up a black army

that by pick and shovel
bare a procession to
the god, Marduk!

Natives cursing and digging
for pay unearth dragons with
upright tails and sacred bulls
alternately
in four tiers
lining the way to an old altar!
Natives digging at old walls
digging me warmth, digging me
sweet loneliness
high enamelled walls.

IV

My second spring
passed in a monastery
with plaster walls in Fiesole
on the hill above Florence.

My second spring painted
a virgin, in a blue aureole
sitting on a three-legged stool,
arms crossed
she is intently serious,
and still
watching an angel
with coloured wings
half kneeling before her
and smiling, the angel's eyes
holding the eyes of Mary
as a snake's holds a bird's.
On the ground there are flowers,
trees are in leaf.

V

But! now for the battle!
Now for murder, now for the real thing!
My third springtime is approaching!
Winds!
lean, serious as a virgin,
seeking, seeking the flowers of March.

Seeking
flowers nowhere to be found,
they twine among the bare branches
in insatiable eagerness
they whirl up the snow

seeking under it
they, the winds, snakelike
roar among yellow reeds
seeking flowers, flowers.

I spring among them
seeking one flower
in which to warm myself!

I deride with all the ridicule
of misery
my own starved misery.

Counter-cutting winds
strike against me
refreshing their fury!

Come, good, cold fellows!
Have we no flowers?
Defy then with even more
desperation than ever, being
lean and frozen!

But though you are lean and frozen
think of the blue bulls of Babylon.

Fling yourselves upon
their empty roses
cut savagely!

But
think of the painted monastery
at Fiesole.

BERKET AND THE STARS

A day on the boulevards chosen out of ten years of
student poverty! One best day out of ten good ones.
Berket in high spirits "Ha, oranges! Let's have one!"
And he made to snatch an orange from the vender's cart.

Now so clever was the deception, so nicely timed
to the full sweep of certain wave summits,
that the rumor of the thing has come down through
three generations, which is relatively forever!

A CELEBRATION

A middle-northern March, now as always
gusts from the south broken against cold winds
but from under, as if a slow hand lifted a tide,
it moves, not into April, into a second March,
the old skin of wind-clear scales dropping
upon the mould: this is the shadow projects the tree
upward causing the sun to shine in his sphere.

So we will put on our pink felt hat, new last year!
newer this by virtue of brown eyes turning back
the seasons and let us walk to the orchid-house,
see the flowers will take the prize to-morrow
at the Palace.
Stop here, these are our oleanders.
When they are in bloom
You would waste words
It is clearer to me than if the pink
were on the branch. It would be a searching in
a coloured cloud to reveal that which now, huskless,
shows the very reason for their being.

And these the orange-trees, in blossom, no need
to tell with this weight of perfume in the air.
If it were not so dark in this shed one could better
see the white.
It is that very perfume
has drawn the darkness down among the leaves.
Do I speak clearly enough?
It is this darkness reveals that which darkness alone
loosens and sets spinning on waxen wings
not the touch of a finger-tip, not the motion
of a sigh. A too heavy sweetness proves
its own caretaker.
And here are the orchids!
Never having seen
such gaiety I will read these flowers for you:
This is an odd January, died in Villon's time.
Snow, this is and this the stain of a violet
grew in that place the spring that foresaw its own doom.

And this, a certain July from Iceland:
a young woman of that place
breathed it toward the south. It took root there.
The colour ran true but the plant is small.

This falling spray of snowflakes is
a handful of dead Februarys
prayed into flower by Rafael Arevalo Martinez
of Guatemala.
Here's that old friend who

went by my side so many years: this full, fragile
head of veined lavender. Oh that April
that we first went with our stiff lusts
leaving the city behind, out to the green hill
May, they said she was. A hand for all of us:
this branch of blue butterflies tied to this stem.

June is a yellow cup I'll not name; August
the over-heavy one. And here are
russet and shiny, all but March. And March?
Ah, March
Flowers are a tiresome pastime.
One has a wish to shake them from their pots
root and stern, for the sun to gnaw.

Walk out again into the cold and saunter home
to the fire. This day has blossomed long enough.
I have wiped out the red night and lit a blaze
instead which will at least warm our hands
and stir up the talk.
I think we have kept fair time.
Time is a green orchid.

APRIL

If you had come away with me
into another state
we had been quiet together.
But there the sun coming up
out of the nothing beyond the lake was
too low in the sky,
there was too great a pushing
against him,
too much of sumac buds, pink
in the head
with the clear gum upon them,
too many opening hearts of
lilac leaves,
too many, too many swollen
limp poplar tassels on the
bare branches!
It was too strong in the air.
I had no rest against that
springtime!
The pounding of the hoofs on the
raw sods
stayed with me half through the night.
I awoke smiling but tired.

Go to sleep, though of course you will not
to tideless waves thundering slantwise against
strong embankments, rattle and swish of spray
dashed thirty feet high, caught by the lake wind,
scattered and strewn broadcast in over the steady
car rails! Sleep, sleep! Gulls' cries in a wind-gust
broken by the wind; calculating wings set above
the field of waves breaking.
Go to sleep to the lunge between foam-crests,
refuse churned in the recoil. Food! Food!
Offal! Offal! that holds them in the air, wave-white
for the one purpose, feather upon feather, the wild
chill in their eyes, the hoarseness in their voices
sleep, sleep....

Gentlefooted crowds are treading out your lullaby.
Their arms nudge, they brush shoulders,
hitch this way then that, mass and surge at the crossings
lullaby, lullaby! The wild-fowl police whistles,
the enraged roar of the traffic, machine shrieks:
it is all to put you to sleep,
to soften your limbs in relaxed postures,
and that your head slip sidewise, and your hair loosen
and fall over your eyes and over your mouth,
brushing your lips wistfully that you may dream,
sleep and dream

A black fungus springs out about lonely church doors
sleep, sleep. The Night, coming down upon
the wet boulevard, would start you awake with his
message, to have in at your window. Pay no
heed to him. He storms at your sill with
cooings, with gesticulations, curses!
You will not let him in. He would keep you from sleeping.
He would have you sit under your desk lamp
brooding, pondering; he would have you
slide out the drawer, take up the ornamented dagger
and handle it. It is late, it is nineteen-nineteen
go to sleep, his cries are a lullaby;
his jabbering is a sleep-well-my-baby; he is
a crackbrained messenger.

The maid waking you in the morning
when you are up and dressing,
the rustle of your clothes as you raise them
it is the same tune.
At table the cold, greenish, split grapefruit, its juice

on the tongue, the clink of the spoon in
your coffee, the toast odors say it over and over.

The open street-door lets in the breath of
the morning wind from over the lake.
The bus coming to a halt grinds from its sullen brakes
lullaby, lullaby. The crackle of a newspaper,
the movement of the troubled coat beside you
sleep, sleep, sleep, sleep....
It is the sting of snow, the burning liquor of
the moonlight, the rush of rain in the gutters packed
with dead leaves: go to sleep, go to sleep.
And the night passes and never passes

OVERTURE TO A DANCE OF LOCOMOTIVES

I

Men with picked voices chant the names
of cities in a huge gallery: promises
that pull through descending stairways
to a deep rumbling.
The rubbing feet
of those coming to be carried quicken a
grey pavement into soft light that rocks
to and fro, under the domed ceiling,
across and across from pale
earthcoloured walls of bare limestone.

Covertly the hands of a great clock
go round and round! Were they to
move quickly and at once the whole
secret would be out and the shuffling
of all ants be done forever.

A leaning pyramid of sunlight, narrowing
out at a high window, moves by the clock:
disaccordant hands straining out from
a center: inevitable postures infinitely
repeated

II

Two, twofour, twoeight!
Porters in red hats run on narrow platforms.
This way ma'm!
important not to take
the wrong train!
Lights from the concrete
ceiling hang crooked but

Poised horizontal
on glittering parallels the dingy cylinders
packed with a warm glow, inviting entry
pull against the hour. But brakes can
hold a fixed posture till
The whistle!

Not twoeight. Not twofour. Two!

Gliding windows. Colored cooks sweating
in a small kitchen. Taillights

In time: twofour!
In time: twoeight!

rivers are tunneled: trestles
cross oozy swampland: wheels repeating
the same gesture remain relatively
stationary: rails forever parallel
return on themselves infinitely.
The dance is sure.

ROMANCE MODERNE

Tracks of rain and light linger in
the spongy greens of a nature whose
flickering mountain, bulging nearer,
ebbing back into the sun
hollowing itself away to hold a lake,
or brown stream rising and falling
at the roadside, turning about,
churning itself white, drawing
green in over it, plunging glassy funnels
fall
And the other world
the windshield a blunt barrier:
Talk to me. Sh! they would hear us.
the backs of their heads facing us
The stream continues its motion of
a hound running over rough ground.

Trees vanish, reappear, vanish:
detached dance of gnomes as a talk
dodging remarks, glows and fades.
The unseen power of words
And now that a few of the moves
are clear the first desire is
to fling oneself out at the side into
the other dance, to other music.

Peer Gynt. Rip Van Winkle. Diana.

If I were young I would try a new alignment
alight nimbly from the car, Good-bye!
Childhood companions linked two and two
criss-cross: four, three, two, one.
Back into self, tentacles withdrawn.
Feel about in warm self-flesh.
Since childhood, since childhood!
Childhood is a toad in the garden, a
happy toad. All toads are happy
and belong in gardens. A toad to Diana!

Lean forward. Punch the steersman
behind the ear. Twirl the wheel!
Over the edge! Screams! Crash!
The end. I sit above my head
a little removed or
a thin wash of rain on the roadway
I am never afraid when he is driving,
interposes new direction,
rides us sidewise, unforseen
into the ditch! All threads cut!
Death! Black. The end. The very end

I would sit separate weighing a
small red handful: the dirt of these parts,
sliding mists sheeting the alders
against the touch of fingers creeping
to mine. All stuff of the blind emotions.
But, stirred, the eye seizes
for the first time - The eye awake!
anything, a dirt bank with green stars
of scrawny weed flattened upon it under
a weight of air - For the first time!
or a yawning depth: Big!
Swim around in it, through it
all directions and find
vitreous seawater stuff
God how I love you! or, as I say,
a plunge into the ditch. The end. I sit
examining my red handful. Balancing
this - in and out - agh.

Love you? It's
a fire in the blood, willy-nilly!
It's the sun coming up in the morning.
Ha, but it's the grey moon too, already up
in the morning. You are slow.
Men are not friends where it concerns
a woman? Fighters. Playfellows.

White round thighs! Youth! Sighs!
It's the fillip of novelty. It's -

Mountains. Elephants humping along
against the sky indifferent to
light withdrawing its tattered shreds,
worn out with embraces. It's
the fillip of novelty. It's a fire in the blood.

Oh get a flannel shirt, white flannel
or pongee. You'd look so well!
I married you because I liked your nose.
I wanted you! I wanted you
in spite of all they'd say

Rain and light, mountain and rain,
rain and river. Will you love me always?
A car overturned and two crushed bodies
under it. Always! Always!
And the white moon already up.
White. Clean. All the colors.
A good head, backed by the eye - awake!
backed by the emotions - blind
River and mountain, light and rain or
rain, rock, light, trees - divided:
rain-light counter rocks-trees or
trees counter rain-light-rocks or

Myriads of counter processions
crossing and recrossing, regaining
the advantage, buying here, selling there
You are sold cheap everywhere in town!
lingering, touching fingers, withdrawing
gathering forces into blares, hummocks,
peaks and rivers, river meeting rock
I wish that you were lying there dead
and I sitting here beside you.
It's the grey moon, over and over.
It's the clay of these parts.

THE DESOLATE FIELD

Vast and grey, the sky
is a simulacrum
to all but him whose days
are vast and grey, and
In the tall, dried grasses
a goat stirs
with nozzle searching the ground.

my head is in the air
but who am I...?
And amazed my heart leaps
at the thought of love
vast and grey
yearning silently over me.

WILLOW POEM

It is a willow when summer is over,
a willow by the river
from which no leaf has fallen nor
bitten by the sun
turned orange or crimson.
The leaves cling and grow paler,
swing and grow paler
over the swirling waters of the river
as if loath to let go,
they are so cool, so drunk with
the swirl of the wind and of the river
oblivious to winter,
the last to let go and fall
into the water and on the ground.

APPROACH OF WINTER

The half stripped trees
struck by a wind together,
bending all,
the leaves flutter drily
and refuse to let go
or driven like hail
stream bitterly out to one side
and fall
where the salvias, hard carmine,
like no leaf that ever was
edge the bare garden.

JANUARY

Again I reply to the triple winds
running chromatic fifths of derision
outside my window:
Play louder.
You will not succeed. I am

bound more to my sentences
the more you batter at me
to follow you.
And the wind,
as before, fingers perfectly
its derisive music.

BLIZZARD

Snow:
years of anger following
hours that float idly down
the blizzard
drifts its weight
deeper and deeper for three days
or sixty years, eh? Then
the sun! a clutter of
yellow and blue flakes
Hairy looking trees stand out
in long alleys
over a wild solitude.
The man turns and there
his solitary track stretched out
upon the world.

TO WAKEN AN OLD LADY

Old age is
a flight of small
cheeping birds
skimming
bare trees
above a snow glaze.
Gaining and failing
they are buffetted
by a dark wind
But what?
On harsh weed stalks
the flock has rested,
the snow
is covered with broken
seed husks
and the wind tempered
by a shrill
piping of plenty.

WINTER TREES

All the complicated details
of the attiring and
the disattiring are completed!
A liquid moon
moves gently among
the long branches.
Thus having prepared their buds
against a sure winter
the wise trees
stand sleeping in the cold.

COMPLAINT

They call me and I go
It is a frozen road
past midnight, a dust
of snow caught
in the rigid wheeltracks.
The door opens.
I smile, enter and
shake off the cold.
Here is a great woman
on her side in the bed.
She is sick,
perhaps vomiting,
perhaps laboring
to give birth to
a tenth child. Joy! Joy!
Night is a room
darkened for lovers,
through the jalousies the sun
has sent one gold needle!
I pick the hair from her eyes
and watch her misery
with compassion.

THE COLD NIGHT

It is cold. The white moon
is up among her scattered stars
like the bare thighs of
the Police Seargent's wife among
her five children....
No answer. Pale shadows lie upon

the frosted grass. One answer:
It is midnight, it is still
and it is cold...!
White thighs of the sky! a
new answer out of the depths of
my male belly: In April....
In April I shall see again. In April!
the round and perfect thighs
of the Police Sergent's wife
perfect still after many babies.
Oya!

SPRING STORM

The sky has given over
its bitterness.
Out of the dark change
all day long
rain falls and falls
as if it would never end.
Still the snow keeps
its hold on the ground.
But water, water
from a thousand runnels!
It collects swiftly,
dappled with black
cuts a way for itself
through green ice in the gutters.
Drop after drop it falls
from the withered grass-stems
of the overhanging embankment.

THE DELICACIES

The hostess, in pink satin and blond hair dressed
high, shone beautifully in her white slippers against
the great silent bald head of her little-eyed husband!
Raising a glass of yellow Rhine wine in the narrow
space just beyond the light-varnished woodwork and
the decorative column between dining-room and hall,
she smiled the smile of water tumbling from one ledge
to another.

We began with a herring salad: delicately flavoured
saltiness in scallops of lettuce-leaves.

The little owl-eyed and thick-set lady with masses

of grey hair has smooth pink cheeks without a wrinkle.
She cannot be the daughter of the little red-faced
fellow dancing about inviting lion-headed Wolff the
druggist to play the piano! But she is. Wolff is a
terrific smoker: if the telephone goes off at night, so
his curled-haired wife whispers, he rises from bed but
cannot answer till he has lighted a cigarette.

Sherry wine in little conical glasses, dull brownish
yellow, and tomatoes stuffed with finely cut chicken
and mayonnaise!

The tall Irishman in a Prince Albert and the usual
striped trousers is going to sing for us. (The piano
is in a little alcove with dark curtains.) The hostess's
sister, ten years younger than she, in black net and
velvet, has hair like some filmy haystack, cloudy about
the eyes. She will play for her husband.

My wife is young, yes she is young and pretty when
she cares to be, when she is interested in a discussion:
it is the little dancing mayor's wife telling her of the
Day nursery in East Rutherford, 'cross the track,
divided from us by the railroad and disputes as to
precedence. It is in this town the saloon flourishes,
the saloon of my friend on the right whose wife has
twice offended with chance words. Her English is
atrocious! It is in this town that the saloon is situated,
close to the railroad track, close as may be, this side
being dry, dry, dry: two people listening on opposite
sides of a wall! The Day Nursery had sixty-five
babies the week before last, so my wife's eyes shine
and her cheeks are pink and I cannot see a blemish.

Ice-cream in the shape of flowers and domestic
objects: a pipe for me since I do not smoke, a doll
for you.

The figure of some great bulk of a woman disappearing
into the kitchen with a quick look over the
shoulder. My friend on the left who has spent the
whole day in a car the like of which some old fellow
would give to an actress: flower-holders, mirrors,
curtains, plush seats, my friend on the left who is
chairman of the Streets committee of the town council and
who has spent the whole day studying automobile
fire-engines in neighbouring towns in view of
purchase, my friend, at the Elks last week at the
breaking-up hymn, signalled for them to let Bill, a
familiar friend of the saloon-keeper, sing out all alone
to the organ and he did sing!

Salz-rolls, exquisite! and Rhine wine _ad libitum_.
A masterly caviare sandwich.

The children flitting about above stairs. The
councilman has just bought a National eight, some car!

For heaven's sake I mustn't forget the halves of
green peppers stuffed with cream cheese and whole
walnuts!

THURSDAY

I have had my dream, like others
and it has come to nothing, so that
I remain now carelessly
with feet planted on the ground
and look up at the sky
feeling my clothes about me,
the weight of my body in my shoes,
the rim of my hat, air passing in and out
at my nose and decide to dream no more.

THE DARK DAY

A three-day-long rain from the east
an interminable talking, talking
of no consequence - patter, patter, patter.
Hand in hand little winds
blow the thin streams aslant.
Warm. Distance cut off. Seclusion.
A few passers-by, drawn in upon themselves,
hurry from one place to another.
Winds of the white poppy! there is no escape!
An interminable talking, talking,
talking ... it has happened before.
Backward, backward, backward.

TIME THE HANGMAN

Poor old Abner, old white-haired nigger!
I remember when you were so strong
you hung yourself by a rope round the neck
in Doc Hollister's barn to prove you could beat
the faker in the circus and it didn't kill you.

Now your face is in your hands, and your elbows
are on your knees, and you are silent and broken.

TO A FRIEND

Well, Lizzie Anderson! seventeen men and
the baby hard to find a father for!

What will the good Father in Heaven say
to the local judge if he do not solve this problem?
A little two pointed smile and pouff!
the law is changed into a mouthful of phrases.

THE GENTLE MAN

I feel the caress of my own fingers
on my own neck as I place my collar
and think pityingly
of the kind women I have known.

THE SOUGHING WIND

Some leaves hang late, some fall
before the first frost, so goes
the tale of winter branches and old bones.

SPRING

O my grey hairs!
You are truly white as plum blossoms.

PLAY

Subtle, clever brain, wiser than I am,
by what devious means do you contrive
to remain idle? Teach me, O master.

LINES

Leaves are greygreen,
the glass broken, bright green.

THE POOR

By constantly tormenting them
with reminders of the lice in
their children's hair, the
School Physician first
brought their hatred down on him,
But by this familiarity
they grew used to him, and so,
at last,
took him for their friend and adviser.

COMPLETE DESTRUCTION

It was an icy day.
We buried the cat,
then took her box
and set fire to it
in the back yard.
Those fleas that escaped
earth and fire
died by the cold.

MEMORY OF APRIL

You say love is this, love is that:
Poplar tassels, willow tendrils
the wind and the rain comb,
tinkle and drip, tinkle and drip
branches drifting apart. Hagh!
Love has not even visited this country.

EPITAPH

An old willow with hollow branches
slowly swayed his few high bright tendrils
and sang:

Love is a young green willow
shimmering at the bare wood's edge.

DAISY

The dayseye hugging the earth
in August, ha! Spring is
gone down in purple,
weeds stand high in the corn,
the rainbeaten furrow
is clotted with sorrel
and crabgrass, the
branch is black under
the heavy mass of the leaves
The sun is upon a
slender green stem
ribbed lengthwise.
He lies on his back
it is a woman also
he regards his former
majesty and
round the yellow center,
split and creviced and done into
minute flowerheads, he sends out
his twenty rays a little
and the wind is among them
to grow cool there!

One turns the thing over
in his hand and looks
at it from the rear: brownedged,
green and pointed scales
armor his yellow.
But turn and turn,
the crisp petals remain
brief, translucent, greenfastened,
barely touching at the edges:
blades of limpid seashell.

PRIMROSE

Yellow, yellow, yellow, yellow!
It is not a color.
It is summer!
It is the wind on a willow,
the lap of waves, the shadow
under a bush, a bird, a bluebird,
three herons, a dead hawk
rotting on a pole

Clear yellow!
It is a piece of blue paper
in the grass or a threecluster of
green walnuts swaying, children
playing croquet or one boy
fishing, a man
swinging his pink fists
as he walks
It is ladysthumb, forgetmenots
in the ditch, moss under
the flange of the carrail, the
wavy lines in split rock, a
great oaktree
It is a disinclination to be
five red petals or a rose, it is
a cluster of birdsbreast flowers
on a red stem six feet high,
four open yellow petals
above sepals curled
backward into reverse spikes
Tufts of purple grass spot the
green meadow and clouds the sky.

QUEEN-ANN'S-LACE

Her body is not so white as
anemony petals nor so smooth, nor
so remote a thing. It is a field
of the wild carrot taking
the field by force; the grass
does not raise above it.
Here is no question of whiteness,
white as can be, with a purple mole
at the center of each flower.
Each flower is a hand's span
of her whiteness. Wherever
his hand has lain there is
a tiny purple blemish. Each part
is a blossom under his touch
to which the fibres of her being
stem one by one, each to its end,
until the whole field is a
white desire, empty, a single stem,
a cluster, flower by flower,
a pious wish to whiteness gone over
or nothing.

GREAT MULLEN

One leaves his leaves at home
being a mullen and sends up a lighthouse
to peer from: I will have my way,
yellow - A mast with a lantern, ten
fifty, a hundred, smaller and smaller
as they grow more - Liar, liar, liar!
You come from her! I can smell djer-kiss
on your clothes. Ha, ha! you come to me,
you, I am a point of dew on a grass-stem.
Why are you sending heat down on me
from your lantern. You are cowdung, a
dead stick with the bark off. She is
squirting on us both. She has had her
hand on you! Well? She has defiled
ME. Your leaves are dull, thick
and hairy. Every hair on my body will
hold you off from me. You are a
dungcake, birdlime on a fence rail.
I love you, straight, yellow
finger of God pointing to - her!
Liar, broken weed, duncake, you have
I am a cricket waving his antenae
and you are high, grey and straight. Ha!

WAITING

When I am alone I am happy.
The air is cool. The sky is
flecked and splashed and wound
with color. The crimson phalloi
of the sassafrass leaves
hang crowded before me
in shoals on the heavy branches.
When I reach my doorstep
I am greeted by
the happy shrieks of my children
and my heart sinks.
I am crushed.

Are not my children as dear to me
as falling leaves or
must one become stupid
to grow older?
It seems much as if Sorrow
had tripped up my heels.
Let us see, let us see!
What did I plan to say to her

when it should happen to me
as it has happened now?

THE HUNTER

In the flashes and black shadows
of July
the days, locked in each other's arms,
seem still
so that squirrels and colored birds
go about at ease over
the branches and through the air.

Where will a shoulder split or
a forehead open and victory be?

Nowhere.
Both sides grow older.

And you may be sure
not one leaf will lift itself
from the ground
and become fast to a twig again.

ARRIVAL

And yet one arrives somehow,
finds himself loosening the hooks of
her dress
in a strange bedroom
feels the autumn
dropping its silk and linen leaves
about her ankles.
The tawdry veined body emerges
twisted upon itself
like a winter wind...!

TO A FRIEND CONCERNING SEVERAL LADIES

You know there is not much
that I desire, a few crysanthemums
half lying on the grass, yellow
and brown and white, the
talk of a few people, the trees,
an expanse of dried leaves perhaps

with ditches among them.
But there comes
between me and these things
a letter
or even a look, well placed,
you understand,
so that I am confused, twisted
four ways and left flat,
unable to lift the food to
my own mouth:
Here is what they say: Come!
and come! and come! And if
I do not go I remain stale to
myself and if I go
I have watched
the city from a distance at night
and wondered why I wrote no poem.
Come! yes,
the city is ablaze for you
and you stand and look at it.

And they are right. There is
no good in the world except out of
a woman and certain women alone
for certain things. But what if
I arrive like a turtle
with my house on my back or
a fish ogling from under water?
It will not do. I must be
steaming with love, colored
like a flamingo. For what?
To have legs and a silly head
and to smell, pah! like a flamingo
that soils its own feathers behind.
Must I go home filled
with a bad poem?
And they say:
Who can answer these things
till he has tried? Your eyes
are half closed, you are a child,
oh, a sweet one, ready to play
but I will make a man of you and
with love on his shoulder!

And in the marshes
the crickets run
on the sunny dike's top and
make burrows there, the water
reflects the reeds and the reeds
move on their stalks and rattle drily.

YOUTH AND BEAUTY

I bought a dishmop
having no daughter
for they had twisted
fine ribbons of shining copper
about white twine
and made a towsled head
of it, fastened it
upon a turned ash stick
slender at the neck
straight, tall
when tied upright
on the brass wallbracket
to be a light for me
and naked,
as a girl should seem
to her father.

THE THINKER

My wife's new pink slippers
have gay pom-poms.
There is not a spot or a stain
on their satin toes or their sides.
All night they lie together
under her bed's edge.
Shivering I catch sight of them
and smile, in the morning.
Later I watch them
descending the stair,
hurrying through the doors
and round the table,
moving stiffly
with a shake of their gay pom-poms!
And I talk to them
in my secret mind
out of pure happiness.

THE DISPUTANTS

Upon the table in their bowl
in violent disarray
of yellow sprays, green spikes
of leaves, red pointed petals

and curled heads of blue
and white among the litter
of the forks and crumbs and plates
the flowers remain composed.
Cooly their colloquy continues
above the coffee and loud talk
grown frail as vaudeville.

TULIP BED

The May sun whom
all things imitate
that glues small leaves to
the wooden trees
shone from the sky
through bluegauze clouds
upon the ground.
Under the leafy trees
where the suburban streets
lay crossed,
with houses on each corner,
tangled shadows had begun
to join
the roadway and the lawns.
With excellent precision
the tulip bed
inside the iron fence
upreared its gaudy
yellow, white and red,
rimmed round with grass,
reposedly.

THE BIRDS

The world begins again!
Not wholly insufflated
the blackbirds in the rain
upon the dead topbranches
of the living tree,
stuck fast to the low clouds,
notate the dawn.
Their shrill cries sound
announcing appetite
and drop among the bending roses
and the dripping grass.

THE NIGHTINGALES

My shoes as I lean
unlacing them
stand out upon
flat worsted flowers
under my feet.
Nimbly the shadows
of my fingers play
unlacing
over shoes and flowers.

SPOUTS

In this world of
as fine a pair of breasts
as ever I saw
the fountain in
Madison Square
spouts up of water
a white tree
that dies and lives
as the rocking water
in the basin
turns from the stonerim
back upon the jet
and rising there
reflectively drops down again.

BLUEFLAGS

I stopped the car
to let the children down
where the streets end
in the sun
at the marsh edge
and the reeds begin
and there are small houses
facing the reeds
and the blue mist
in the distance
with grapevine trellises
with grape clusters
small as strawberries
on the vines
and ditches

running springwater
that continue the gutters
with willows over them.
The reeds begin
like water at a shore
their pointed petals waving
dark green and light.
But blueflags are blossoming
in the reeds
which the children pluck
chattering in the reeds
high over their heads
which they part
with bare arms to appear
with fists of flowers
till in the air
there comes the smell
of calamus
from wet, gummy stalks.

THE WIDOW'S LAMENT IN SPRINGTIME

Sorrow is my own yard
where the new grass
flames as it has flamed
often before but not
with the cold fire
that closes round me this year.
Thirtyfive years
I lived with my husband.
The plumtree is white today
with masses of flowers.
Masses of flowers
load the cherry branches
and color some bushes
yellow and some red
but the grief in my heart
is stronger than they
for though they were my joy
formerly, today I notice them
and turn away forgetting.
Today my son told me
that in the meadows,
at the edge of the heavy woods
in the distance, he saw
trees of white flowers.
I feel that I would like
to go there
and fall into those flowers

and sink into the marsh near them.

LIGHT HEARTED WILLIAM

Light hearted William twirled
his November moustaches
and, half dressed, looked
from the bedroom window
upon the spring weather.

Heigh-ya! sighed he gaily
leaning out to see
up and down the street
where a heavy sunlight
lay beyond some blue shadows.

Into the room he drew
his head again and laughed
to himself quietly
twirling his green moustaches.

PORTRAIT OF THE AUTHOR

The birches are mad with green points
the wood's edge is burning with their green,
burning, seething. No, no, no.
The birches are opening their leaves one
by one. Their delicate leaves unfold cold
and separate, one by one. Slender tassels
hang swaying from the delicate branch tips
Oh, I cannot say it. There is no word.
Black is split at once into flowers. In
every bog and ditch, flares of
small fire, white flowers! Agh,
the birches are mad, mad with their green.
The world is gone, torn into shreds
with this blessing. What have I left undone
that I should have undertaken

O my brother, you redfaced, living man
ignorant, stupid whose feet are upon
this same dirt that I touch and eat.
We are alone in this terror, alone,
face to face on this road, you and I,
wrapped by this flame!
Let the polished plows stay idle,
their gloss already on the black soil.

But that face of yours!
Answer me. I will clutch you. I
will hug you, grip you. I will poke my face
into your face and force you to see me.
Take me in your arms, tell me the commonest
thing that is in your mind to say,
say anything. I will understand you!
It is the madness of the birch leaves opening
cold, one by one.

My rooms will receive me. But my rooms
are no longer sweet spaces where comfort
is ready to wait on me with its crumbs.
A darkness has brushed them. The mass
of yellow tulips in the bowl is shrunken.
Every familiar object is changed and dwarfed.
I am shaken, broken against a might
that splits comfort, blows apart
my careful partitions, crushes my house
and leaves me with shrinking heart
and startled, empty eyes, peering out
into a cold world.

In the spring I would drink! In the spring
I would be drunk and lie forgetting all things.
Your face! Give me your face, Yang Kue Fei!
your hands, your lips to drink!
Give me your wrists to drink
I drag you, I am drowned in you, you
overwhelm me! Drink!
Save me! The shad bush is in the edge
of the clearing. The yards in a fury
of lilac blossoms are driving me mad with terror.
Drink and lie forgetting the world.

And coldly the birch leaves are opening one by one.
Coldly I observe them and wait for the end.
And it ends.

THE LONELY STREET

School is over. It is too hot
to walk at ease. At ease
in light frocks they walk the streets
to while the time away.
They have grown tall. They hold
pink flames in their right hands.
In white from head to foot,
with sidelong, idle look

in yellow, floating stuff,
black sash and stockings
touching their avid mouths
with pink sugar on a stick
like a carnation each holds in her hand
they mount the lonely street.

THE GREAT FIGURE

Among the rain
and lights
I saw the figure 5
in gold
on a red
firetruck
moving
with weight and urgency
tense
unheeded
to gong clangs
siren howls
and wheels rumbling
through the dark city.

THE TEMPERS

PEACE ON EARTH

The Archer is wake!
The Swan is flying!
Gold against blue
An Arrow is lying.
There is hunting in heaven
Sleep safe till to-morrow.

The Bears are abroad!
The Eagle is screaming!
Gold against blue
Their eyes are gleaming!
Sleep!
Sleep safe till to-morrow.

The Sisters lie
With their arms intertwining;
Gold against blue

Their hair is shining!
The Serpent writhes!
Orion is listening!
Gold against blue
His sword is glistening!
Sleep!
There is hunting in heaven
Sleep safe till to-morrow.

POSTLUDE

Now that I have cooled to you
Let there be gold of tarnished masonry,
Temples soothed by the sun to ruin
That sleep utterly.
Give me hand for the dances,
Ripples at Philae, in and out,
And lips, my Lesbian,
Wall flowers that once were flame.

Your hair is my Carthage
And my arms the bow,
And our words arrows
To shoot the stars
Who from that misty sea
Swarm to destroy us.

But you there beside me
Oh how shall I defy you,
Who wound me in the night
With breasts shining
Like Venus and like Mars?
The night that is shouting Jason
When the loud eaves rattle
As with waves above me
Blue at the prow of my desire.

FIRST PRAISE

Lady of dusk wood fastnesses,
Thou art my Lady.
I have known the crisp splintering leaf-tread with thee on before,
White, slender through green saplings;
I have lain by thee on the grey forest floor
Beside thee, my Lady.

Lady of rivers strewn with stones,

Only thou art my Lady.
Where thousand the freshets are crowded like peasants to a fair;
Clear skinned, wild from seclusion,
They jostle white armed down the tent-bordered thoroughfare
Praising my Lady.

HOMAGE

Elvira, by love's grace
There goeth before you
A clear radiance
Which maketh all vain souls
Candles when noon is.

The loud clangour of pretenders
Melteth before you
Like the roll of carts passing,
But you come silently
And homage is given.

Now the little by-path
Which leadeth to love
Is again joyful with its many;
And the great highway
From love
Is without passers.

THE FOOL'S SONG

I tried to put a bird in a cage.
O fool that I am!
For the bird was Truth.
Sing merrily, Truth: I tried to put
Truth in a cage!

And when I had the bird in the cage,
O fool that I am!
Why, it broke my pretty cage.
Sing merrily, Truth; I tried to put
Truth in a cage!

And when the bird was flown from the cage,
O fool that I am!
Why, I had nor bird nor cage.
Sing merrily, Truth: I tried to put
Truth in a cage!
Heigh-ho! Truth in a cage.

From "THE BIRTH OF VENUS," Song

Come with us and play!
See, we have breasts as women!
From your tents by the sea
Come play with us: it is forbidden!

Come with us and play!
Lo, bare, straight legs in the water!
By our boats we stay,
Then swimming away
Come to us: it is forbidden!

Come with us and play!
See, we are tall as women!
Our eyes are keen:
Our hair is bright:
Our voices speak outright:
We revel in the sea's green!
Come play:
It is forbidden!

IMMORTAL

Yes, there is one thing braver than all flowers;
Richer than clear gems; wider than the sky;
Immortal and unchangeable; whose powers
Transcend reason, love and sanity!

And thou, beloved, art that godly thing!
Marvellous and terrible; in glance
An injured Juno roused against Heaven's King!
And thy name, lovely One, is Ignorance.

MEZZO FORTE

Take that, damn you; and that!
And here's a rose
To make it right again!
God knows
I'm sorry, Grace; but then,
It's not my fault if you will be a cat.

AN AFTER SONG

So art thou broken in upon me, Apollo,
Through a splendour of purple garments
Held by the yellow-haired Clymène
To clothe the white of thy shoulders
Bare from the day's leaping of horses.
This is strange to me, here in the modern twilight.

CRUDE LAMENT

Mother of flames,
The men that went ahunting
Are asleep in the snow drifts.
You have kept the fire burning!
Crooked fingers that pull
Fuel from among the wet leaves,
Mother of flames
You have kept the fire burning!
The young wives have fallen asleep
With wet hair, weeping,
Mother of flames!
The young men raised the heavy spears
And are gone prowling in the darkness.
O mother of flames,
You who have kept the fire burning!
Lo, I am helpless!
Would God they had taken me with them!

THE ORDEAL

O Crimson salamander,
Because of love's whim
sacred!
Swim
the winding flame
Predestined to disman him
And bring our fellow home to us again.

Swim in with watery fang,
Gnaw out and drown
The fire roots that circle him
Until the Hell-flower dies down
And he comes home again.

Aye, bring him home,

O crimson salamander,
That I may see he is unchanged with burning
Then have your will with him,
O crimson salamander.

THE DEATH OF FRANCO OF COLONGE. HIS PROPHECY OF BEETHOVEN

It is useless, good woman, useless: the spark fails me.
God! yet when the might of it all assails me
It seems impossible that I cannot do it.
Yet I cannot. They were right, and they all knew it
Years ago, but I - never! I have persisted
Blindly (they say) and now I am old. I have resisted
Everything, but now, now the strife's ended.
The fire's out; the old cloak has been mended
For the last time, the soul peers through its tatters.
Put a light by and leave me; nothing more matters
Now; I am done; I am at last well broken!
Yet, by God, I'll still leave them a token
That they'll swear it was no dead man writ it;
A morsel that they'll mark well the day they bit it,
That there'll be sand between their gross teeth to crunch yet
When goodman Gabriel blows his concluding trumpet.
Leave me!
And now, little black eyes, come you out here!
Ah, you've given me a lively, lasting bout, year
After year to win you round me darlings!
Precious children, little gambollers! "farlings"
They might have called you once, "nearlings"
I call you now, I, first of all the yearlings,
Upon this plain, for I it was that tore you
Out of chaos! It was I bore you!
Ah, you little children that go playing
Over the five-barred gate, and will still be straying
Spite of all that I have ever told you
Of counterpoint and cadence which does not hold you
No more than chains will for this or that strange reason,
But you're always at some new loving treason
To be away from me, laughing, mocking,
Witlessly, perhaps, but for all that forever knocking
At this stanchion door of your poor father's heart till - oh, well
At least you've shown that you can grow well
However much you evade me faster, faster.
But, black eyes, some day you'll get a master,
For he will come! He shall, he must come!
And when he finishes and the burning dust from
His wheels settles - what shall men see then?
You, you, you, my own lovely children!
Aye, all of you, thus with hands together

Playing on the hill or there in a tether,
Or running free, but all mine! Aye, my very namesakes
Shall be his proper fame's stakes.
And he shall lead you!
And he shall meed you!
And he shall build you gold palaces!
And he shall wine you from clear chalices!
For I have seen it! I have seen it
Written where the world-clouds screen it
From other eyes
Over the bronze gates of paradise!

PORTENT

Red cradle of the night,
In you
The dusky child
Sleeps fast till his might
Shall be piled
Sinew on sinew.

Red cradle of the night,
The dusky child
Sleeping sits upright.
Lo how
The winds blow now!
He pillows back;
The winds are again mild.

When he stretches his arms out,
Red cradle of the night,
The alarms shout
From bare tree to tree,
Wild
In afright!
Mighty shall he be,
Red cradle of the night,
The dusky child!!

CON BRIO

Miserly, is the best description of that poor fool
Who holds Lancelot to have been a morose fellow,
Dolefully brooding over the events which had naturally to follow
The high time of his deed with Guinevere.
He has a sick historical sight, if I judge rightly,
To believe any such thing as that ever occurred.

But, by the god of blood, what else is it that has deterred
Us all from an out and out defiance of fear
But this same perdamnable miserliness,
Which cries about our necks how we shall have less and less
Than we have now if we spend too wantonly?

Bah, this sort of slither is below contempt!

In the same vein we should have apple trees exempt
From bearing anything but pink blossoms all the year,
Fixed permanent lest their bellies wax unseemly, and the dear
Innocent days of them be wasted quite.

How can we have less? Have we not the deed?

Lancelot thought little, spent his gold and rode to fight
Mounted, if God was willing, on a good steed.

AD INFINITUM

Still I bring flowers
Although you fling them at my feet
Until none stays
That is not struck across with wounds:
Flowers and flowers
That you may break them utterly
As you have always done.

Sure happily
I still bring flowers, flowers,
Knowing how all
Are crumpled in your praise
And may not live
To speak a lesser thing.

TRANSLATIONS FROM THE SPANISH, "EL ROMANCERO"

I

Although you do your best to regard me
With an air seeming offended,
Never can you deny, when all's ended,
Calm eyes, that you _did_ regard me.

However much you're at pains to
Offend me, by which I may suffer,
What offence is there can make up for
The great good he finds who attains you?

For though with mortal fear you reward me,
Until my sorry sense is plenished,
Never can you deny, when all's ended,
Calm eyes, that you did regard me.

Thinking thus to dismay me
You beheld me with disdain,
But instead of destroying the gain,
In fact with doubled good you paid me.
For though you show them how hardly
They keep off from leniency bended,
Never can you deny, when all's ended,
Calm eyes, that you did regard me.

II
Ah, little green eyes,
Ah, little eyes of mine,
Ah, Heaven be willing
That you think of me somewise.

The day of departure
You came full of grieving
And to see I was leaving
The tears 'gan to start sure
With the heavy torture
Of sorrows unbrightened
When you lie down at night and
When there to you dreams rise,
Ah, Heaven be willing
That you think of me somewise.

Deep is my assurance
Of you, little green eyes,
That in truth you realise
Something of my durance
Eyes of hope's fair assurance
And good premonition
By virtue of whose condition
All green colours I prize.
Ah, Heaven be willing
That you think of me somewise.

Would God I might know you
To which quarter bended
And why comprehended
When sighings overflow you,
And if you must go through
Some certain despair,
For that you lose his care
Who was faithful always.

Ah, Heaven be willing
That you think of me these days.

Through never a moment
I've known how to live lest
All my thoughts but as one pressed
You-ward for their concernment.
May God send chastisement
If in this I belie me
And if it truth be
My own little green eyes.
Ah, Heaven be willing
That you think of me somewise.

III

Poplars of the meadow,
Fountains of Madrid,
Now I am absent from you
All are slandering me.

Each of you is telling
How evil my chance is
The wind among the branches,
The fountains in their welling
To every one telling
You were happy to see.
Now I am absent from you
All are slandering me.

With good right I may wonder
For that at my last leaving
The plants with sighs heaving
And the waters in tears were.
That you played double, never
Thought I this could be,
Now I am absent from you
All are slandering me.

There full in your presence
Music you sought to waken,
Later I'm forsaken
Since you are ware of my absence.
God, wilt Thou give me patience
Here while suffer I ye,
Now I am absent from you
All are slandering me.

IV

The day draweth nearer,

And morrow ends our meeting,
Ere they take thee sleeping
Be up - away, my treasure!

Soft, leave her breasts all unheeded,
Far hence though the master still remaineth!
For soon uptil our earth regaineth
The sun all embraces dividing.
N'er grew pleasure all unimpeded,
N'er was delight lest passion won,
And to the wise man the fit occasion
Has not yet refused a full measure:
Be up - away, my treasure!

If that my love thy bosom inflameth
With honest purpose and just intention,
To free me from my soul's contention
Give over joys the day shameth;
Who thee lameth he also me lameth,
And my good grace builds all in thy good grace;
Be up - away! Fear leaveth place,
That thou art here, no more unto pleasure,
Be up - away, my treasure!

Although thou with a sleep art wresting,
'Tis rightful thou bringst it close,
That of the favour one meeting shows
An hundred may hence be attesting.
'Tis fitting too thou shouldst be mindful
That the ease which we lose now, in kind, full
Many a promise holds for our leisure;
Ere they take thee sleeping;
Be up - away, my treasure!

HIC JACET

The coroner's merry little children
Have such twinkling brown eyes.
Their father is not of gay men
And their mother jocular in no wise,
Yet the coroner's merry little children
Laugh so easily.

They laugh because they prosper.
Fruit for them is upon all branches.
Lo! how they jibe at loss, for
Kind heaven fills their little paunches!
It's the coroner's merry, merry children
Who laugh so easily.

CONTEMPORANIA

The corner of a great rain
Steamy with the country
Has fallen upon my garden.

I go back and forth now
And the little leaves follow me
Talking of the great rain,
Of branches broken,
And the farmer's curses!

But I go back and forth
In this corner of a garden
And the green shoots follow me
Praising the great rain.

We are not curst together,
The leaves and I,
Framing devices, flower devices
And other ways of peopling
The barren country.

Truly it was a very great rain
That makes the little leaves follow me.

TO WISH MYSELF COURAGE

On the day when youth is no more upon me
I will write of the leaves and the moon in a tree top!
I will sing then the song, long in the making
When the stress of youth is put away from me.

How can I ever be written out as men say?
Surely it is merely an interference with the long song
This that I am now doing.

But when the spring of it is worn like the old moon
And the eaten leaves are lace upon the cold earth
Then I will rise up in my great desire
Long at the birth and sing me the youth-song!

WILLIAM CARLOS WILLIAMS – A CONCISE BIBLIOGRAPHY

Poetry Collections
Poems (1909)
The Tempers (1913)
Al Que Quiere! (1917)
Sour Grapes (1921)
Spring and All (1923)
Go Go (1923)
The Cod Head (1932)
Collected Poems, 1921-1931 (1934)
An Early Martyr and Other Poems (1935)
Adam & Eve & The City (1936)
The Complete Collected Poems of William Carlos Williams, 1906-1938 (1938)
The Broken Span (1941)
The Wedge (1944)
Paterson Book I (1946); Book II (1948); Book III (1949); Book IV (1951); Book V (1958)
Clouds, Aigeltinger, Russia (1948)
The Collected Later Poems (1950)
Collected Earlier Poems (1951)
The Desert Music and Other Poems (1954)
Journey to Love (1955)
Pictures from Brueghel and Other Poems (1962)

Books, Prose
Kora in Hell: Improvisations (1920)
The Great American Novel (1923)
Spring and All (1923)
In the American Grain (1925)
A Voyage to Pagany (1928)
Novelette and Other Prose (1932)
The Knife of the Times, and Other Stories (1932)
White Mule (1937)
Life along the Passaic River (1938)
In the Money (1940)
Make Light of It: Collected Stories (1950)
Autobiography (1951)
The Build-Up (1952)
Selected Essays (1954)
The Selected Letters of William Carlos Williams (1957)
I Wanted to Write a Poem: The Autobiography of the Works of a Poet (1958)
Yes, Mrs. Williams: A Personal Record of My Mother (1959)
The Farmers' Daughters: Collected Stories (1961)
Imaginations (1970) - A collection of five previously published early works.
The Embodiment of Knowledge (1974)
Interviews with William Carlos Williams: "Speaking Straight Ahead" (1976)
A Recognizable Image: William Carlos Williams on Art and Artists (1978)
William Carlos Williams: The Doctor Stories - compiled by Robert Coles" (1984)
Pound/Williams: Selected Letters of Ezra Pound and William Carlos Williams (1996)
The Collected Stories of William Carlos Williams (1996)
The Letters of Denise Levertov and William Carlos Williams (1998)
William Carlos Williams and Charles Tomlinson: A Transatlantic Connection (1998)
The Humane Particulars: The Collected Letters of William Carlos Williams and Kenneth Burke (2004)

www.ingramcontent.com/pod-product-compliance
Lightning Source LLC
Chambersburg PA
CBHW060059050426
42448CB00011B/2536